CW00819907

Graphology (Teach Yourself)

Yourself)

How To Use Handwriting Analysis To Uncover A Person's Darkest Secrets

Table of Contents

Introduction

Imagine if there were a method for discovering the secret information that the people you encounter in your day-to-day life keep hidden from you. Would you be intrigued enough to find out more?

We all know people who wear their hearts on their sleeves, their life is an open book, and with the rise in popularity of mediums such as social media, some people provide us with what has come to be known as 'too much information' on, what can seem to be, a minute-by-minute basis.

However, the truth is, the majority of people are much more complex than they may at first appear to be. You know this to be true of yourself, and, if you can be entirely honest, you're probably happy to agree that we all, to some extent, have a public face and a private face.

So what if there were some way to get to the very heart of people you know, to find out what makes them tick, to uncover their true personality?

Imagine if you could find out if a person:

- May be lying about something

- Can't be trusted with money

- Is more narrow-minded than they may at first appear

- Has a strong work ethic or is likely to be lazy

- Is reliable

- Might be cheating on you

- Suffers from mood swings

- Is disorganized

- Keeps their emotions well-hidden

Would you like to be able to create psychological profiles of colleagues, friends, acquaintances, partners or potential partners to uncover the personality traits they may be hiding from you?

As you are about to find out, there is a way to do this...

1. What is graphology?

The art of graphology, or handwriting analysis, offers us the opportunity to uncover secret information about the deeper inner workings of people's personalities.

Graphology is best described as the study of graphic movement, such as handwriting and doodles, and it is used to analyze the human personality.

Through graphology, it's possible to gain an incisive insight into a person's physical, mental and emotional state. Understanding the principles of graphology can give you the edge when it comes to understanding the secret motivations and concealed thoughts of your friends and your enemies!

How did graphology begin?

The study of handwriting appears to have its roots in the 17th century. It's widely believed that an Italian doctor of medicine and philosophy, called Camillo Baldi, published the first book on handwriting analysis in 1622.

The term graphology first appeared in the 1870s when a Frenchman, Jean Michon, published his many years of research on the subject. As a result of Michon's work, interest in graphology began to spread throughout Europe, to the extent that the psychology departments of many respected universities began to offer graphology Masters and Ph.D. degrees in graphology.

Interest in graphology as a psychological science continued to spread through Europe and to the United States in the early part of the 19th century, and today graphology is still used, for a variety of reasons, in many parts of the world.

What can graphology reveal about a person?

Graphology can reveal a surprising amount of information about a person. A skilled graphologist is able to uncover psychological information relating to a person's intellect, temperament, motivations, aptitudes, reliability, attitudes and interpersonal skills, simply by analyzing a piece of their handwriting.

What is graphology used for?

Graphology is used by many different organizations worldwide for many different reasons. Whenever it's important to understand people in greater depth, graphology can provide an added and intriguing insight into the human personality. It can also be used in your own life, to understand yourself better, or to help you to understand partners, colleagues or children.

One of the most well known uses for graphology is found in the field of Recruitment and Human Resources. Graphologists analyze the handwriting of prospective candidates for jobs to create a shortlist of suitable applicants for large businesses and organizations.

Graphology is also sometimes used to help solve crime. A veritable rogues gallery of murderers, thieves, rapists, fraudsters, spies, arsonists, petty crooks and criminals have all been pinned down by the secrets they gave away via their handwriting.

How does graphology work?

Our hands do not determine the style of our writing, so whether a person is left-handed or right-handed is of no importance in graphology. The way in which we write is determined by our brains, and this why graphologists believe that by considering the style of a person's handwriting, we can understand their character in greater depth.

This is best reflected in the way in which our handwriting changes as we grow from childhood to adulthood. Just as our personalities change and mature with age, so too does our writing style. Our handwriting provides a graphologist with a mirror of what is happening in our brains; our character, emotions, intelligence and inner thoughts are reflected in the way we write - precisely because writing comes from the brain.

Is graphology foolproof?

The answer to this question is probably no. It's possible for people to disguise their handwriting if they really want to, although many experienced graphologists believe that it's impossible to disguise handwriting for a prolonged period of time. This is why longer writing samples are more beneficial when it comes to analyzing handwriting; people are likely to revert to some, if not all, of their true writing style eventually.

There are other factors that can affect handwriting style. You may be thinking that your own writing is inconsistent, and this means that a graphologist won't be able to build up a true picture of your personality – an inconsistent writing style is common in many people.

If you're writing in a rush, it makes sense that your handwriting will look a little different to how it does when you're concentrating hard and want your writing to look its best. A skilled graphologist can work out when you're writing in a hurry and when you're taking greater care. In fact, even with an untrained eye there are easy, logical ways to spot this difference.

The surface a person writes on and the instrument they use to write can also affect handwriting style and these things need to be taken into consideration when it comes to analyzing handwriting.

If handwriting reflects personality can a person change their handwriting to change their personality?

Some people do believe that this is possible. This branch of graphology is known as graphotherapy. The theory behind graphotherapy is that by changing the handwriting, it's possible to rewire the brain. Some people use graphotherapy to 'teach' their brain how to concentrate better, others use it to help them learn to relax. There are a variety of ways that graphology can be used but the desired outcome is always the same – to enable the person to be more effective, productive or successful in the way they most desire to be.

Unlocking the secrets of personality with graphology

So what do graphologists look for when they analyze a piece of handwriting? How can you find out if someone is lying to you, or if a person can be trusted or not? How do serial killers and other criminals give themselves away? In the next chapter, we'll take a look at how graphologists uncover the sensitive secrets and the hidden truths people unwittingly reveal through the style of their writing.

2. How handwriting is analyzed

"Handwriting can infallibly show whether it comes from a person who is noble-minded or from one who is vulgar".

Confuscius

Have you ever met a person and instantly thought "I don't like the look of him" only to be proven completely wrong in your judgment of that person at a later date?

It's fair to say that we all make judgments about people based on the way they look, but, the fact is, appearances can be deceptive. We all know that we shouldn't judge a book by its cover.

Handwriting analysis, on the other hand, is a surprisingly accurate tool when it comes to assessing the characteristics of a person. A graphologist is able to assess a person's intelligence, energy levels and emotional state just by looking at their handwriting.

The ability to analyze handwriting is held in such regard that the FBI and the CIA are reported to have built extensive psychological profiles of some of the world's most notorious criminals using expert knowledge provided by professional graphologists. Graphologists have also revealed the true authors of poison pen letters and forgeries to help solve crime.

Many large companies use handwriting analysis to help them choose the best candidates for employment, weeding out potentially lazy or dishonest candidates by assessing their handwriting. Graphology is also utilized in the field of genealogy to understand how people in the past - historical figures and our ancestors - behaved.

How can a graphologist know so much?

As we have already mentioned, handwriting comes from the brain and not the hand. Graphologist's, therefore, view handwriting as "brainwriting." Whenever a person writes, they leave an imprint of the goings on in their brain, indelibly on the piece of paper they wrote on, providing graphologists with a sort of x-ray of a person's mind. This reveals how a person thinks, feels and behaves - essentially, our handwriting reveals who we truly are.

Once we have learned how to write, the brain takes over and writing becomes something that is automatic to us, something that we do unconsciously. We develop our own writing style without really thinking about it, and it is this style that reflects our true nature.

Sometimes, if we want to put more effort into our writing we do engage our brains. This is when we *do* write consciously, for example, if you have to handwrite an application form, or want to make sure that your writing is completely legible, you may put in extra, conscious effort.

So, a person's handwriting can be a mix of both conscious and unconscious style. A trained graphologist is able to spot the difference between the two and analyze both styles. In graphology, conscious writing helps a graphologist to understand a person's conscious mind and unconscious writing helps them to uncover a person's unconscious mind.

Personality traits you can and can't change

As human beings, each individual's personality is made up of fixed and unfixed traits. Fixed traits are the aspects of personality that we are either born with, or that we develop as a result of our early experiences related to our environment, influences and education. These include:

- IQ

- Identity

- Aptitudes

- Temperament

Unfixed personality traits are changeable; the environment, the people that we work alongside, further study of a subject, can alter them. We all know that we can wake up one day feeling stressed out, unmotivated and fed up. A few days later, however, we may feel fantastic and ready to take on the world. Our feelings and behavior are often subject to change. Unfixed traits include:

- Mood

- Ability

- Attitude

- Beliefs

- Motivation level

- State of physical health

If you were asked to pick your own handwriting out of 100 handwriting samples you could probably do it. This is because a part of your own unique handwriting style never changes. Your moods and beliefs may change at times, but a part of your personality always remains the same.

How graphologists dig out your deepest secrets

Deciphering handwriting is a matter of detective work. Graphologists pick up on five basic clues that people give away about the workings of their mind in their handwriting. Graphologists do this by:

- Making common sense judgments

- Looking for physiological giveaways

- Understanding widely accepted concepts

- Using empirical research

- Using psychological knowledge

So, let's take a look at each of these techniques to see how graphologists get to the very heart of a person.

Common sense

The easiest clues to pick up about a person from their handwriting are the obvious things that immediately stand out when you look at a piece of hand written content.

For example, it is easy to tell if someone is illiterate from his or her handwriting. A person with a low level of literacy will make frequent spelling mistakes and grammatical errors, such as not using periods, capitalizing in the wrong places and not capitalizing when necessary. Their handwriting may be untidy or difficult to read and they may not know how to use the space well on paper, or how to construct sentences.

Physiological giveaways

People give away clues about the state of their health through their handwriting. For example, it is possible to tell if a person was under the influence of drugs or alcohol at the time they wrote as their handwriting is likely to be sprawling and illegible.

It's also possible to tell if a person suffers with a medical condition from their handwriting; individuals with conditions that affect their fine motor skills, such as Parkinson's disease, learning disabilities and stammering may share similar handwriting traits.

Accepted Concepts

Graphologists also consider widely accepted concepts when they analyze a piece of handwriting. They use this technique to understand the emotional state of mind and the personality traits of the writer.

If a person is angry at the time they write, they may press down onto the paper more firmly. A person who is feeling "down" at the time of writing may produce text that slopes down the page, and a person who is unconventional in personality my have a very unique writing style that is unlike the handwriting of people who hold more traditional views on life.

Empirical Research

Empirical research is the process of collecting evidence by study. Graphologists have studied large numbers of handwriting samples to help them understand common traits. So, for example, the handwriting of a large group of people with above average IQ can be studied to see if these people share any common writing traits. The same studies have been carried out on other groups, such as convicted criminals and violent schizophrenics.

Psychology

Knowledge of psychology also plays a part in the analysis of handwriting. Someone who is not being truthful may exaggerate certain words they write, so they appear to be bigger than other words in the text. This can indicate that the person is trying to convince others that something is true when it isn't.

Putting it all together

When analyzing handwriting, it is important not to reach conclusions by only analyzing one piece of a person's writing. It is much better if you can analyze several pieces of their writing and even better if those samples have been collected over an extended period of time i.e. they were not written on the same day.

The following chapters will show you how to analyze a person's handwriting using the techniques that professional graphologists' use. The aim is to provide you with some of the basics so that you can begin to understand people on a deeper level, and reveal the secrets they give away via their handwriting.

3. Writing Zones

The zones

In graphology there are three zones. These are known as the upper zone, the middle zone and the lower zone.

The upper zone relates to the mind. Handwriting that reaches up into this zone can tell us about a person's spiritual, philosophical or intellectual interests; it also relates to fantasies, dreams and ideas.

The middle zone relates to the ego – a person's view of him or herself. Handwriting in this zone can tell us about a person's everyday life; their level of commons sense, their state of mind at the time they wrote and the way a person sees him or herself in relation to others.

The lower zone relates to the subconscious mind. Handwriting that reaches into this zone can tell us about a person's instincts and desires. We can find out about their attitudes towards health, money and sex by observing handwriting that falls into this zone.

Zone balance

In graphology a healthy adult would display handwriting that falls predominately, but not exclusively, in the middle zone. Writing in the upper zone – for example when capitalizing – should be exactly the same height as when reaching into the lower zone – for example when using letters that use the lower zone such a p and y.

Of course, most people don't maintain a perfect balance all the time and this is only a general rule. Writing size varies all the time, sometimes consciously at other times unconsciously, depending on a person's mood, so it is important to take this into consideration when analyzing a piece of handwriting.

Dominant upper zone

Some types of handwriting reach into the upper zone frequently. Writing that shows upper zone dominance will be taller, fuller or more elaborate in the upper parts of a piece of writing.

Upper zone dominance reveals a number of traits, some positive, some negative and some that are open to interpretation.

Positive	Open	Negative
Ambitious	Lack of inhibition	Fantasist
Leadership qualities	Proud	Impractical

Courageous	Fearless	Extravagant
Adventurous	Free spirit	Egotistical
Generous	Creative	Selfish

Handwriting traits of the upper zone

Loops and stress

Loops in the upper zone are found on letters such as b, d, f, h, k, l, and t. Loops that are pointed in shape can show a tendency towards Type A personality behaviors such as a predisposition towards stress, tension, anxiety and frustration.

The emotions that are revealed in this handwriting trait relate to constriction. A loop that is considered to be normal will be slightly rounded - if a loop is angular or pointed, we can deduce that the person writing feels stressed or anxious in some way.

Retraced loops and lies

Retraced loops are created when the writer retraces a stem, making it appear thicker or bolder than other parts of their writing. Frequent use of retraced stems can indicate that a person is lying, although this one example is not 100% foolproof; there are other handwriting traits that need to be taken into consideration to be sure that someone isn't telling the truth.

When writing naturally, loops may occur as a matter of course but if a person is trying their hardest to conceal something, their writing will be more intense – hence the retraced loops. In trying to hold something back, tension is created within the handwriting and retracing upper zone strokes is one such example of this. It is generally thought that if over 35% of a person's upper zone strokes are retraced, there's a good chance that they might not be telling the truth.

Broken loops and fragile emotions

Broken loops occur when the hand leaves the paper and, when found in both the upper and lower zones, can represent the fragile state of mind of the writer. Marilyn Monroe's later handwriting is said to have contained many broken loops.

If a piece of writing contains many broken loops it may reveal a fragile or broken emotional state of mind; as the letters seem to be falling apart so too is the writer.

Balloons and loss of reality

Balloon shaped or very rounded loops in the upper zone can represent a psychotic nature. However, it is **vital**, that you do not make this diagnosis of anyone who displays this handwriting trait; it has been included here as a matter of interest only.

Balloon shaped loops are created when the loop crosses at a high point and can show that a person does not have a good handle on reality - as the handwriting is distorted, so too is the mind.

Dominant middle zone

Writing that frequently remains in the middle zone lacks higher and lower strokes that reach into the upper and lower zones.

Middle zone dominance shows a number of positive and negative personality traits.

Positive	Negative
Sociable	Immature
Home-loving	Concerned with outward appearance
Light-hearted	Lack of depth

Handwriting traits of the middle zone

Small middle zone and unhappiness

Small-sized writing that shrinks well into the middle zone can indicate unhappiness and anxiety. The smaller the writing, or the more poorly it is formed, the unhappier the person that has written it. If a person feels unhappy or anxious, for whatever reason, their writing may become restricted, there is a lack of flow and a lack of expansion.

To be able to deduce that this is a long-term problem, you would need to analyze a series of handwriting samples from the same person over a period of time. But if a person's writing is squashed, poorly formed or uneven in the middle zone it may be that at the time they wrote, they were feeling unhappy.

Well-formed middle zone and concentration

People who display neat, well-formed writing in the middle zone may also be showing their ability for above average concentration levels. Researchers, scientists, writers and bookkeepers often display this handwriting tendency.

The ability to concentrate for long periods of time is given away by small, clear writing that falls predominantly in the middle zone.

Dominant lower zone

Writing that shows dominance in the lower zone displays deeper strokes and flourishes in the bottom parts of a piece of handwriting.

Lower zone dominance shows a number of positive and negative personality traits.

Positive	Negative
Down-to-earth	Materialistic
Ambitious	Hidden worries
Open to new ideas	Insecurity

Handwriting traits of the lower zone

Long strokes and restlessness

Loops in the lower zone are found on letters such as f, g, j, p, q and y. Long strokes and loops that occur in the lower zone can indicate a restless nature. A writer who frequently makes use of the lower zone may be displaying their need for constant change and variety, and the lower the loop or stroke reaches, the more intense the need for change is in that person.

People who frequently change their job or move house or location a number of times may display this tendency. When it comes to assessing whether one person is better for a job than another, this is the writing trait that could give away the level of your reliability or for sticking to something for a long period of time.

Large lower zone loops and urges

Large loops in lower zone letters can indicate a lack of something in the writer's life. Quite often the lack may relate to money, but a more positive way of interpreting this is that maybe the feeling of lacking is what drives this person towards working hard for material success.

It is also thought that large lower loops can indicate a higher than average sex drive. But if you want to be able to spot sexual deviancy, you need to look for loops that are reversed, for example, the hook on a letter y wouldn't curl to the left, it would flick back to the right.

4. Slants and directions

What is slant?

The "slant" in graphology is perhaps the easiest part of handwriting to define – basically a person's handwriting will slant to the left, the right or remain upright in the middle.

Writing with a slant to the right is very common, partly because many of us were taught to write this way in school, but also because most languages are written from the left of a page and across to the right; it simply feels more natural to slant to the right when holding a pen in hand. The fact that more people are right-handed than left-handed also contributes to right slant dominance.

Slanting to the left is less natural, but there are many people who do it and graphologists look out for this idiosyncrasy in handwriting to gather their evidence. Surprisingly enough, writing with a slant to the left is not something that is only found in left-handed writers, many left-slanting writers are right-handed.

As there is no evidence to suggest a physical reason for people slanting their writing to the left, graphologists have deduced that the reason for this must be psychological, i.e. caused by the state of mind or the emotions.

How to measure slant

There are four main types of writing slant:

Reclining slant: Leans to the left

Upright: No slant

Forward slant: Leans to the right

Irregular slant: Slants randomly to the left or the right

In graphology, slant is measured by examining the angle that is created by the down strokes in a piece of writing in relation to the baseline. The baseline is sometimes referred to as the writing line; this simply means the line on which the letters of a person's handwriting sit. This measurement can be taken using a ruler and protractor to give you a degree measurement.

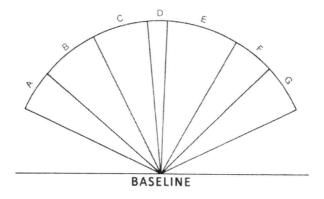

BASELINE

The diagram above gives you an idea about how far slants can reach in writing. In analyzing handwriting using this method, graphologists make the following conclusions:

Slant to the left

The visual image of handwriting that slants to the left gives away some immediate clues about the writer. As the writing leans back, so too does the personality of the writer. This is a person who may tend to live in the past, who holds themselves back from the limelight and from other people.

Interestingly, many teenagers experiment with a leftwards slant before reverting back to the more natural forwards slant. The reason behind this could be because of the fact that teenagers notoriously experience strong hormonal changes. This handwriting tendency could reveal inner, emotional turmoil or the need to rebel against their parents as part of the natural separation process that occurs between parents and their children during the teenage years.

Analysis of handwriting that slopes to the left is generally quite negative. Even the positive traits that left slanted writing suggest are ambiguous and could be described as negative.

Positive	Negative
Contemplative	Excessive shyness

Introspective	Insecure
Self-sacrificing	Immature
Rich inner-life	Reserved
Independent	Trauma in early life or past

A = Strong recline

A person that displays a strong slant to the left in their writing may repress their emotions, much more so than most people do. They avoid dealing with their emotions at all costs and sometimes at a cost to their well-being.

They have a tendency to live in their mind or in their own world. This person may dwell on past events and have regrets about the way their life has turned out. They are generally introverts and may be self-obsessed. Sometimes they are overly concerned with material gain or outward appearances.

B = Medium recline

A person that displays a medium slant to the left in their handwriting is also liable to repress their emotions but to a lesser extent than those that display a strong leftwards slant. These people may appear to be cold, aloof and self-sufficient, they are generally not the easiest of people to get along with.

C = Slight recline

A slight slant to the left in handwriting is, perhaps, the least negative of the three types in the left-slanting group. Many people are introverted and reserved emotionally without it impacting too much on their life, or on the lives of the people close to them. People with this hand writing trait may seem cool and detached; they cannot be described as straightforward people and may take some time to warm up and get to know.

D = Upright or no slant

Handwriting that remains straight up and down, without slanting to the left or the right is referred to as upright. This handwriting trait is associated with a need for stability and a diplomatic nature.

People with this trait are, generally, people who are in control of their lives and who live firmly in the present, without any strong leanings towards the past or the future.

Positive	Negative
Thinking over feeling	Cold
Diplomatic	Unsympathetic
Lives in the here and now	Indifferent

Reasonable	Detached
In control of their emotions	Cautious
Discriminating	Undemonstrative

Slant to the right

As with the leftwards slant, the visual image of handwriting slanting to the right gives away some immediate clues for the graphologist to pick up on. A right or forwards slant gives an indication that the writer is someone that looks forwards; they lean towards people rather than away from them.

This is the most common slant found in handwriting and more people display this handwriting trait than the left slant and the upright style put together.

Positive	Negative
Sociable and expressive	Impulsive
Affectionate	Lack of will-power
Altruistic	Lives in the future too much
Sympathetic	Heart over head
Interested in others	Highly strung

Energetic and active	Escapist
Visionary	Over-sensitive

E = Slight forward slant

A slight forward slant is perhaps the most preferable of all the slants found in handwriting analysis. The person with this handwriting trait is generally stable, even-tempered and displays appropriate and healthy emotional responses to the positive and negative life events we all encounter. These people express their feelings moderately, they are able to show emotion, unlike those with the left slant preference but they do not go over the top with their emotional responses.

F = Medium forward slant

If a person's handwriting has a reasonably strong slants to the right, they are likely to be the type of person that wears their heart on their sleeve, and generally affectionate, friendly and caring by nature.

These people are ruled more by the heart than by the head, and this can lead them into trouble at times, as they can make unwise choices that haven't been thought through properly. They are likely to have a sensitive nature and may be hurt easily by harsh words, or by people who are more direct or forthright in nature.

G = Strong forward slant

A very strong forward slant can indicate that a person is excessively emotional and maybe not always have control over their emotional state. These people can be overly romantic and gushing in nature, they are often talkative, nervous, oversensitive and easily hurt or offended.

They can come across to others as being highly-strung and may be prone to outbursts of anger, tears and other emotion. The best word to describe this kind of person is volatile – their emotions can be all over the place, up or down from one minute to the next - they are not always the easiest of people to get a long with because of this.

Irregular slant

The term irregular slant is used to describe the handwriting of a person that slants, at random, to both the left and the right. There appears to be no reason for this irregularity, as different words and letters will slope one way at different times throughout the piece of writing.

As you have probably guessed, this type of random slanting suggests that a person is very disorganized, unpredictable and unstable. These people often have a great deal of nervous energy and their lifestyle and general behavior is likely to be erratic and undisciplined.

As is the handwriting, so the personality. This style of writing denotes the kind of person who is pulled in many different directions, so this type of writer is likely to be fickle, changeable and capricious. They will find it difficult to see things through and may be good at beginning projects but not so good at finishing them. These people may also lack common sense and good judgment, which means they could make mistakes or bad choices in their lives if they are not careful.

Direction

Direction, in graphology, refers to how the writing slopes upwards or downwards on the page. To assess direction in a piece of handwriting, the graphologist looks to the baseline. The baseline, as we have already mentioned, is the line where the letters of a piece of writing sit. When people write on lined paper it is easier to assess the direction of the writing; when unlined paper is used the graphologist needs to interpret the information by visualizing the baseline.

Direction in handwriting is, of all the handwriting traits, the most susceptible to change. The speed at which the piece of writing was created, the importance of the subject matter, and the state of mind of the writer are all factors that can alter the direction of handwriting. So, when assessing direction, it's important to know if the upward or downward slope in a person's handwriting is a constant feature, or simply something that is susceptible to change.

Graphologists usually assess direction by creating a line in pencil directly below the middle zone letters. This helps them to see if the handwriting has:

- Rising lines

- Falling lines

- Straight lines

- Wavy lines

- Arcs – concave or convex

Rising lines

Lines that rise in direction throughout a piece of handwriting can indicate the following personality traits.

Positive	Negative
Ambitious	Excessively excitable nature
Optimistic	Irritable

Cheerful nature	Hot-tempered/aggressive

Falling lines

Lines that fall or slope downwards in direction can point towards the following traits:

Positive	Negative
Down to earth nature	Pessimism
Easy going	Apathy and indifference
Critical thinker	Tiredness/fatigue
	Tendency towards depression or repressed anger

Straight lines

Lines that remain straight show a person that is in control, this writing trait can also indicate the following:

Positive	Negative
Constancy	Inflexibility
Self-discipline	Rigid thinking

Strong will power	Straight-laced
Realistic	Prudishness

Wavy lines

Wavy lines tend to look snake-like rather than untidy or irregular. The following personality traits are indicated:

Positive	**Negative**
Diplomatic	Secretive
Emotionally controlled	Passive-aggressive

Arcs

Arcs can be formed when writing direction curves inwards (concave) or curves outwards (convex). The following personality traits are indicated.

Concave	**Convex**
Fighting spirit	Good starter but may not see things through
Ability to make a come back	Easily disappointed

Courage in the face of adversity	Easily bored – like variety
Determination	Gives up easily
Stamina	Lack of stamina/staying power

5. Sizing and spacing in graphology

Size

In graphology, as you have probably guessed, size is assessed by how big or small handwriting appears when written on a page. Size in handwriting style is usually classed as being small, medium or large, but graphologists will also look to see if the size of a person's writing remains the same throughout a piece of writing.

Writing size can give away clues as to how introverted or extroverted that person is or was feeling at the time they wrote; it can also reveal something about an individual's concentration levels.

Size in handwriting is something that is variable. Sometimes the mood of the person affects the size of their writing, at other times it may be that the space the person has to write on has a bearing on writing size, for example, we are all likely to use smaller letters when we're writing on a postcard.

Writing of medium size is considered to be the norm; most people have medium sized writing, so we will examine the larger and smaller types of writing as these traits have more revealing information to offer the graphologist.

Large writing

Positive	Negative
Extrovert	Inability to concentrate
Ambitious	Attention seeking
Leaders	Egotistical
Generous	Extravagant

People with large writing are generally considered to be extroverts, they are the kind of people who like to be noticed and this is reflected in their large, and therefore noticeable, writing style. A person who uses large lettering wants to show the world how great they, rightly or wrongly, think they are; they want to set themselves apart from 'average people' who display more regular, medium sized handwriting.

A large writing style can also suggest a flamboyant nature and may be found in performers, wannabe celebrities and those individuals who seem a little eccentric to others. Large writing is their way of crying out "notice me", and some people who write in this way could definitely be described as show offs. This handwriting trait is often found in actors, politicians and anyone with the gift of the gab, such as successful salespeople!

A positive side to the person with large handwriting is their ability to think big; these people are ambitious and often able to see the bigger picture. They may be visionaries with fantastic ideas, however, they are quite often the kind of people who are good at starting projects but not finishing them. Their inability to concentrate for long periods of time let's them down, but if they are allowed to develop their ideas and put other people to work for them, they may be capable of achieving something quite remarkable.

A note on very large writing

When it comes to large writing, there is large and then there is *very* large! If you come across this type of writing, then all of the above traits will still be true but they will be magnified to a greater extent. This type of writing is found in someone that probably has a loud voice, loud opinions and an extremely healthy view of themselves, perhaps bordering on excess egotism. These people may, however, be deluded and have an over-inflated opinion of themselves.

The truth is, that someone with overly large writing may be trying to convince himself or herself that they are greater than they actually are, and this could stem from deep-rooted insecurity. They may over-do their handwriting to compensate for the fact that, deep inside, they feel small in some way.

A person with very large handwriting is likely to have a poor level of concentration; it's a trait that is sometimes seen in individuals that suffer from hyperactivity disorders. These people also like to draw attention to themselves; people who are considered to be exhibitionists may also display this handwriting trait.

Small writing

Positive	Negative
Modest	Shy or feels inferior
Accurate	Melancholic
Self-disciplined	Petty
Objective	Intolerant
Realistic	Rigid thinking

A person with small writing is likely to be introverted, the size of their writing reflects their need to stay contained within their own space – they are not the kind of people to reach out to others, or who want to be the center of attention.

Introversion is not necessarily a negative trait, and it may well be that a person with small writing is just one of those people who is very self-contained. Some people do not need the constant attention or approval of other people to be happy.

However, some people with small handwriting may be excessively shy, or they may have some sort of inferiority complex. The fact that their handwriting shrinks away, reflects their tendency to shrink away from other people or from pushing themselves forwards in work situations for example. These people may not be able to achieve their potential because of their inability to be bold or to believe in themselves.

On a more positive note, many exceptional scientists, mathematicians, writers and composers have small handwriting. This is because small handwriting also reflects an enhanced ability for concentration. Interestingly most of these professions require that the person spend a lot of time alone – a natural trait very often found in those with small handwriting.

A note on very small writing

Writing that is miniscule in size represents an extreme of personality, in the same way that we found with very large handwriting. The above personality traits will all be magnified in a person with very small handwriting. Academics and intellectuals may produce very small handwriting, reflecting their ability to concentrate, focus and think at a profound level.

If a person's handwriting changes over a period of time, from being average sized to small, it may be important to observe that person - especially if they are a child, teenager or young adult. Writing that shrinks over time can indicate that all is not well with that person, they may be sinking into depression, or something else may be troubling them. Handwriting that diminishes in size over a period of time suggests that the writer is retreating into him or herself in some way.

Space

In graphology, space relates to the distance found between the words and letters in a piece of handwriting. The use of space is assessed to determine a person's level of intelligence, the way they relate to other people, and how they behave socially.

Wide writing

If a person's handwriting looks 'wide' on the page, it shows a love for freedom and expansion, this may be someone who doesn't want to conform – a free–spirit perhaps? These people are generally sociable and outgoing but their relationships may lack any real depth, they may also be the kind of people who talk or gossip too much.

Writing that looks 'wide' on the page, is generally believed to represent the following personality traits.

Positive	Negative
Open-minded	Inconsiderate
Adventurous – enjoys travel	Talkative
Freedom-loving	Extravagant
Sincere	Lack of self-discipline
Unconventional	Speaks before thinking

Wide spacing between words

When an individual uses wide spacing between words the effects are very noticeable on paper. This style of writing is immediately noticeable and stands out from the page.

The person who writes in this way likes to keep other people at arm's length, even though they may crave the attention and approval of others in some way. These people are suspicious of others and find it hard to trust anyone. It would be difficult to have a close or intimate relationship with a person that displays this handwriting trait.

Another reason for this is that people with this handwriting trait need a lot of space and freedom; they need to be on the go and hate to be tied down to one person or one place. This handwriting trait is often seen in those who have the traveling bug, those with a nomadic soul, and those who do not want to settle down to live conventional lives or have close or conventional relationships with others.

Wide spacing between individual letters

If the spacing between individual letters is wide, this will also immediately stand out to a graphologist. This is an unusual handwriting trait that is not seen in many people at all. This handwriting trait can be found in people who feel socially isolated from others, they may not be able to relate to other people very well at all and will come across as detached from others.

Narrow writing

When a person displays a writing style that appears narrow on the page, it shows some sense of restriction and a need for control. People with this handwriting trait are more likely to avoid interaction with others and avoid social situations.

Positive	Negative
Self-disciplined	Inhibited

Self-control	Narrow minded
Considerate	Shy
Thrifty and economical	Anxious or fearful

Narrow spacing between words

When each word is placed closely next to the other in a sample of writing, it shows that the writer may hold a very narrow view of the world. They may think in a limited way and not be open to new ideas or possibilities.

The inability to put enough space between words also shows up in people who lack the ability to understand social space. We have all met the kind of person who stands too close to us during a conversation and recognize how strangely uncomfortable this can feel. People who do not understand social boundaries such as this may display this handwriting trait.

Narrow spacing between individual letters

Writing that appears squashed together, because there is little space between each individual letter, reveals an uptight personality. This is the handwriting trait of people who do not like to open up to others and who find it difficult to relax in social situations.

6. Pressure, margins and fullness

Pressure

Pressure, in graphology, refers to the amount of force used when writing. Basically, it relates to how hard or how soft you apply your pen or pencil to paper.

From writing pressure, graphologists can work out how tense or relaxed a person is; they can also deduce how they use their mental abilities. And even more interestingly, pressure can tell a graphologist about a person's innermost desires.

The amount of pressure used in handwriting is something that is variable, for example, it can depend on your present mood, so graphologists interpret pressure to assess how a person was feeling at the time they wrote. To fully understand a person, you would need to examine the pressure they use in a variety of their writing samples taken over a longer period of time.

In graphology, pressure falls into one of five categories:

- Very light

- Light

- Heavy

- Very heavy

- Irregular/uneven

Very light

Very light pressure in handwriting can indicate a person who has a weak nature, they may be timid, lack energy, have no will-power and no ideas of their own. These people lack courage and are followers, never leaders. They can be easily led into trouble by other, stronger, characters.

Light

Light pressure in handwriting can indicate that the person was feeling generally benign at the time of writing. They were not experiencing any strong feelings one way or another, and were probably feeling quite calm when they wrote. People sometimes adopt this trait when they are feeling content, or even when they are feeling spiritual or connected to their surroundings in a spiritual way.

Heavy

When handwriting shows a strong level pressure, it suggests that the person was feeling energetic, alert and assertive at the time they wrote. When a person writes in this way, they have to contract their muscles and use extra force; this sense of purpose and muscle contraction is carried over into their writing style.

If a person regularly uses heavy pressure, it denotes an active personality; this is someone who is determined and assertive, but also someone who maybe likes to exert power over others.

Very heavy

When the pressure used to write is extremely heavy, so much so that it may tear the paper, this denotes that all is not well. The writer that exerts forceful, heavy pressure is extremely frustrated in some way, and they may also be feeling aggressive or violent. This is a person to be very wary of.

Irregular

If the pressure a person uses varies from light to heavy, or any shade in between, throughout a piece of their handwriting, you could be dealing with someone who is very worried. Irregular use of pressure indicates worrying, nervousness and anxiety.

<u>Margins</u>

Margins are created when a person writes on a blank piece of paper. In graphology, where a person creates their margins reveals how that person interacts with people, and each margin represents a part of that person's whole life to date.

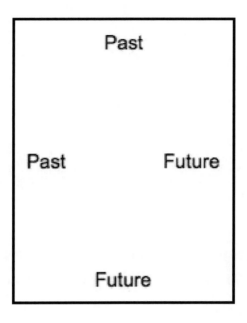

As we write from left to write, the left side of the page represents the past and the right side of the page the future. And as we write from the top of a page to the bottom, the top of the page represents the past and the bottom the future.

Even margins

The left margin on a page is the easiest to control because this is the point from where we begin to write. The right margin is more difficult to control because it isn't possible to predict the length of the last word we can fit onto each line.

A person who manages to control their right margin, along with the left margin, keeping it even throughout a piece of writing is, clearly, someone who is able to concentrate well and plan ahead.

These people are obviously very visually oriented, and aesthetics or appearances may be important to them. It is as if they view the paper they are writing on as a piece of art and want to create something that looks visually attractive.

Designers, artists and those involved in the beauty industry may all display this handwriting trait.

Wide left margin

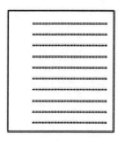

As we have discovered, the left side of the page represents the past, so a person who avoids this part of the page may be trying to escape their past in some way. This handwriting trait is often found in people who have survived traumatic events in the past and indicates their need to move away from their memories of the event.

Wide right margin

People who leave a wide margin to the right may be nervous or fearful about the future. Sometimes these people create imaginary restrictions around themselves because of their lack of belief in themselves. These people may have dreams but, for whatever reason, not be able to see them through.

Wide margins all over

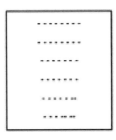

If a person leaves wide margins all around their writing, it shows a need for self-protection. This type of handwriting indicates that a person has built a wall around himself or herself, and either they want to keep people out because they aren't very sociable, or they are too afraid to let people get close to them.

Large upper margin

Writing that begins lower down the page indicates formality, we often begin letters by writing further down the page and this habit extends elsewhere. It is as if we want to show a form of respect to someone else by beginning our writing further down the page.

Large lower margin

This trait provides another indication that a person is fearful in some way about their future and that they are unable to forge forwards to achieve their goals or dreams.

No margins

When no margins are created it can indicate that the person was trying to squeeze a lot of information on to one piece of paper, but when there is no practical reason for a person to use the page so fully i.e. they had more paper available to them, it can point towards a restless personality.

This is the handwriting trait of somebody who needs to fill every minute of his or her life with something to do. Workaholics and those who find it difficult to just sit and be will often display this trait. Interestingly, this trait can also be the sign of a miser or penny-pincher, someone who likes to get their money's worth out of everything – even a piece of paper!

Fullness

Fullness is used to describe how rounded, or how lean, a person's letters look. Full writing generally has a very rounded appearance, with the round letters such as a, b, d, g, o, p and q having a fat or full appearance, some people also use circles to dot their letter i. Lean writing is the exact opposite of this, and will appear as tall and thin writing on the page.

Full writing is generally associated with the following personality traits:

Positive	Negative
Creative	Unrealistic
Vivacious	Self-oriented
Lover of life	Day-dreamer
Optimistic	Scattered thinking

Lean writing is generally associated with the following personality traits:

Positive	Negative
Objective	Pedantic
Focused	Unimaginative

| Realistic outlook | Rigid thinking |

7. Deception and graphology: Spotting liars, criminals and emotional instability through graphology

One of the most interesting uses for graphology is the study of the handwriting of people, and in particular criminals, from history to see if they gave clues away about the dark side of their nature via their handwriting.

Handwriting and murderous tendencies

The following is a list of handwriting traits that point towards a very disturbed mind. We've included this list out of interest only, so it's important that you don't try to diagnose somebody as a serial killer using it!

Handwriting can be used to identify the kind of personality disorders that many serial killers suffer from, but it cannot be used alone, obviously a thorough medical assessment is needed to make any kind of diagnosis of this nature and this is, without a doubt, best left to the professionals!

Strong, heavy pressure	Very angular appearance
Narrow spacing between	Frequent use of the upper and

letters	lower zones
No margins, covering the whole page	Broken letters
Very wide spaces between words	Deep slant to the left
Large writing or emphasizing words	Very weak strokes/pressure
Twisted letters	Alternate use of printed and joined up letters
Lack of punctuation or too much punctuation	Irregularities or unnecessary additions of any kind in size, slant etc.

Notorious serial killers and their handwriting

Charles Manson: Notorious killer and leader of his own cult known as 'The Family', Manson was tried and found guilty of seven murders in 1969. His handwriting displays fewer personality disorder traits than other serial killers, but there are strange flourishes and unnecessary lines added to his writing that give away something of his egotistical tendencies.

Douglas Clark – The Sunset Strip Killers: Along with his accomplice, Carol Bundy, Clark murdered six people in Los Angeles. His handwriting displays sharp angles, irregularities in the lower zone, and words that are emphasized randomly.

Gerald Stano: Stano was executed by electric chair in 1988 after he confessed to killing over 30 women; it is thought that he may have murdered up to 41 women. Abandoned by his natural mother as a baby, Stano's handwriting is extremely sharp and knife-like; he also created strange, irregular shapes with loops in his writing, reflecting his unconventional and disordered outlook on life.

John Wayne Gacy: Serial killer Gacy was convicted of 33 murders and sentenced to death by lethal injection for 12 of these. His handwriting shows wide spacing between words, prominence in the lower zone and loops that twist backwards in the letters that reach the lower zone.

Jeffrey Dahmer: Dahmer was a serial killer whose murders involved dismemberment, cannibalism and necrophilia. A sample of his handwriting shows an extremely warped mind, with most of the negative handwriting traits in the above box found in his writing style.

Roy Norris: Norris, along with Lawrence Bittaker, was one half of the notorious 'Toolbox Killers' convicted of murdering five women. While Bittaker remains on Death Row, Norris was spared the death sentence in return for testifying against Bittaker. Norris's handwriting is extremely narrow and slants backwards to the left. He uses an excessive amount of punctuation, pressure and emphasizes certain words by underlining them. His handwriting is said to look 'frozen' in style, rigid and lacking in any kind of movement, reflecting the cold, calculating mind of a serial killer.

Ted Bundy: Bundy was one of America's most well known serial killers. Before his execution he confessed to some 30 murders, all of which were women, although the total is believed to be much higher. Bundy's handwriting style shows many irregularities in the way he formed his letters and also a deep prominence toward the lower zone.

Zodiac Murders: The Zodiac Murders took place in California in the late 1960s to early 1970s. As yet, no one has been convicted of these killings. The killer sent letters to several local newspapers, which he claimed contained a code for working out his true identity. The killer went on to send more letters containing his unique signature, a circle and cross symbol, from 1970 through to 1974. The writing is childish, words were frequently misspelled and wide spacing between each word is used.

Famous cases where handwriting was used to help solve crime

Ted Bundy Case – Bundy carried out his killings of over 30 women over seven different states in America, so it is easy to understand why investigators did not immediately link a series of murders that occurred between 1974 and 1978. While some serial killers put a 'trademark' stamp on their killings, Bundy did not, further confusing the investigation process. He would use different disguises to ensnare victims and used different methods to kill them.

During one investigation when Bundy had placed a handwritten note on the victim's body, a member of the investigative team remembered hearing about a murder in another state where the same thing had happened. This enabled investigators in both states to compare the handwriting found on the notes. With a match being made, it became clear that they needed to concentrate on finding one serial killer rather than a number of killers. Bundy's handwriting can therefore be credited with one of the early factors that led to his capture.

Josef Mengele Case – Josef Mengele, also known as the Angel of Death, was a German physician at Auschwitz, the Nazi concentration camp where many atrocities were committed. After the war, he escaped being convicted of war crimes by changing his identity and fleeing to South America where he was able to live out his life without ever being caught.

He may have been able to change his identity and his location but his handwriting never changed, and in 1985, after a number of handwriting samples were matched, the remains of a Wolfgang Gerhard were exhumed in Brazil. DNA tests confirmed his identity, but once again it was the man's handwriting that gave him away, proving that handwriting is indeed brainwriting i.e. something we cannot consciously change.

The Salamander Letter Case – The Salamander Letter was one of several letters that surfaced in the early part of the 1980s, said to have been written by Joseph Smith, the founder of the Latter Day Saint movement. This particular letter presented a view of the origins of the movement that was directly at odds with Smith's commonly accepted version.

The letter caused much debate both inside and outside the Latter Day Saint movement and shook the movements' very foundations. However, handwriting analysts, amongst others, were able to prove that this and other letters were clever forgeries. The writer was Mark Hoffman, a young man who had been responsible for discovering many of the letters, including The Salamander Letter. Considered to be one of America's most accomplished forgers, Hoffman is presently serving a life imprisonment for murder and forgery.

Conclusion

Whose handwriting should I analyze?

It's important that you only analyze the handwriting of someone who intended for their words to be read by others. Someone who is writing something that only they will need to interpret or read, may write in a very different way for himself or herself than they would when writing for others.

Now that you have some basic graphology skills you can try interpreting the handwriting of your friends and family, if they are willing to let you do so. You could also try to analyze the handwriting of famous people, past and present. It's possible to find handwriting samples on the internet or in autobiographies and biographies.

How many handwriting samples do I need to be able to analyze someone?

It is always better to have several samples available when it comes to analyzing a person's handwriting. It is also better if these have been written over a period of time, at least over a week, so that you can build up a more accurate profile of the person whose handwriting you wish to analyze.

Using just one sample can lead you to inaccurate conclusions. The writer may have been ill at the time they wrote, or under the influence of alcohol, and if this was so, you won't be getting a true version of their usual handwriting style.

The more writing samples you have from any one individual the better, however, sometimes this is not possible and you may only be able to make your analysis using one, single writing sample. If this is the case, be sure to take extra care when coming to any conclusions about the person you're attempting to analyze.

How do I develop my graphology skills?

We hope that you have enjoyed this introductory guide to the fascinating art of graphology, and as you have probably already guessed, graphology is a skill that will always benefit from further, in-depth study.

It's important that you read as much as possible around the subject, in order to practice, hone and master you budding skills. We promise that once you get truly stuck in to the subject you'll become hooked!

Some people choose to take a course in graphology, in order to be able to offer their services as a professional graphologist and there are several graphology societies operating in a variety of countries around the world if you would like to find out how to develop and enhance your skills as a graphologist.

A word on common sense

An understanding of graphology does not qualify you or anyone, even an expert, to make a personality diagnosis of another person. It is important that you use your new-found skills wisely, and if you attempt to analyze your friends or family that you deliver any information to them sensitively.

Always keep in mind that there may be a variety of reasons as to why a person's handwriting looks the way it does on a sample – there are always various possibilities – telling your good-hearted, old grandmother that her handwriting displays 'serial killer' tendencies is certainly not advised!

As with anything in life, practice makes perfect and it may take a while before you begin to accurately analyze people using graphology. Eventually, and with experience, many of the rules of graphology will become second nature to you and your own intuition will begin to kick in, helping you to get to the very heart of the hidden, most secret and truest traits of the people around you.

We wish you good luck on your graphology journey!

33270226R00039

Printed in Great Britain
by Amazon